BEETLES

by Sophie Lockwood

Content Adviser: Michael Breed, Ph.D., Professor,
Ecology and Evolutionary Biology,
The University of Colorado, Boulder

THE CHILD'S WORLD®, MANKATO, MINNESOTA

Beetles

Published in the United States of America by The Child's World®
1980 Lookout Drive • Mankato, MN 56003-1705
800-599-READ • www.childsworld.com

Acknowledgements:

The Child's World®: Mary Berendes, Publishing Director

The Creative Spark: Mary Francis, Project Director; Wendy Mead, Editor; Deborah Goodsite, Photo Researcher

The Design Lab: Kathleen Petelinsek, Designer, Production Artist, and Cartographer

Photos:

Cover and half title: Bruce Coleman Inc./Alamy; frontispiece and CIP: Witold Ryka/iStockphoto.com.

Interior: Corbis: 29 (Sandro Vannini); Getty Images: 12 (Davies & Starr/Stone), 14, 16 (George Grall/National Geographic); iStockphoto.com: (Agita Leimane) 26; Minden Pictures: 5, 9 (Tom Vezo), 5, 30, 32 (Stephen Dalton), 5, 36 (Mitsuhiko Imamori); Oxford Scientific: 5, 11, 25 (Satoshi Kuribayashi), 8 (Michael Fogden), 21 (Oxford Scientific); Photo Researchers, Inc.: 19 (Scott Camazine), 22 (Eye of Science), 34 (George D. Lepp).

Map: The Design Lab: 7.

Library of Congress Cataloging-in-Publication Data

Lockwood, Sophie.
 Beetles / by Sophie Lockwood.
   p. cm.—(The world of insects)
 Includes index.
 ISBN-13: 978-1-59296-819-0 (library bound: alk. paper)
 ISBN-10: 1-59296-819-8 (library bound: alk. paper)
 1. Beetles—Juvenile literature. I.Title.
 QL576.2.L63 2007
 595.76—dc22   2006103459

TABLE OF CONTENTS

Chapter One

A Battle of Rhinos

In a small village in a Thailand jungle, men gather for an evening's entertainment. The men have brought their prized male rhinoceros beetles with them to pit the strength of one beetle against another. As the men form a circle, two male rhino beetles confront each other. The battle is fierce with each beetle trying to push the other over. Tonight's winner has been champion several times, and its owner is delighted. This is a natural behavior for rhino beetles—the way males attract females in the wild.

Rhino beetles live mostly in tropical rainforests, although some are found in North America. Rhinoceros beetles—although fierce when fighting their own species—tend to be shy and harmless. Active at night, hidden in the day, these large beetles scurry under fallen leaves or rotting trees branches. Rhino beetles feed on rotting fruit or tree sap and do not eat much of these items considering their size. Rhino beetles measure between 2.5 and 6 centimeters (1 to 2.5 inches)—fairly large for beetles.

Did You Know?
For its size, a rhino beetle is the strongest animal in the world. It can carry up to 850 times its own weight. As strong as an elephant is, it could not carry 850 other elephants or their equivalent weight.

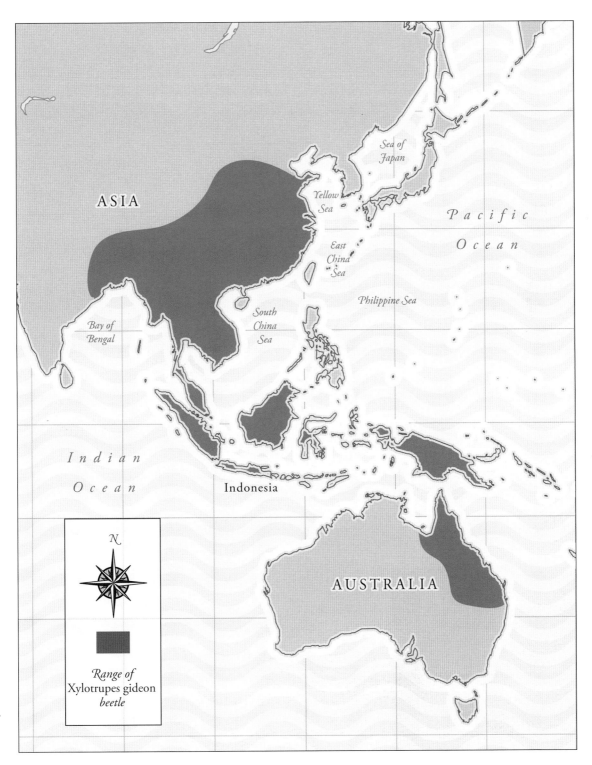

While the species of rhinoceros beetle known as Xylotrupes gideon *lives primarily in Asia, other types of rhino beetles can be found on almost every continent.*

It is mating season. The males search the forest floor for a top-quality feeding site. It is not their own food they seek but a food source for their future young. The males engage in battle to attract the females. The winner pushes the loser off a branch or stone, secures the feeding territory, and wins the female.

Females want to mate with strong males so that they can produce strong young. After mating, females lay their eggs in rotting wood or rotting leaves on the forest floor. The eggs hatch, and tiny **larvae** emerge. The larvae eat and eat and eat—devouring the rotting wood or compost in which they live. Rhinoceros beetle

Would You Believe?
When rhino beetles are under stress, they hiss or squeak. The noise, hopefully, chases off predators.

Two male rhino beetles fight as a part of their mating ritual.

larvae go through three stages of development called instars. As they grow, the larvae cast off their too-small skins in a process called molting.

The larvae fill themselves with food until they are bulging. They dig cells in the soil that they line with **feces**. The cell meets the needs of the **pupae**. The larvae undergo a change of body form, from a wormlike creature to a hard-shelled beetle.

Some rhino beetles have become serious pests in tropical lands. The adults lay eggs in stalks of sugarcane or the hearts of tender young palms. Both food sources are tasty treats, and countries that grow these products for crops struggle to keep the beetles under control.

In some countries, rhino beetles are considered to be pests.

Chapter Two

The Beetle Cycle of Life

Biologists have discovered that every continent, every island, and every major body of fresh water has one thing in common—beetles. There are more species of beetles than any other kind of insect on Earth, coming in a variety of colors, shapes, and sizes. Long-horned beetles (*Titanus giganteus)* measure up to 18 centimeters (7 inches) long— about the length of a human hand. Other beetle species are so small that they can only be seen by using a special type of microscope.

BODY PARTS

Beetles are typical insects with three main body parts: a head, a **thorax**, and an **abdomen**. Beetle heads include mouths, brains, **antennae**, compound eyes, and, possibly, horns and snouts. Mouthparts are critical for beetles because they provide a means of eating. The size and shape of the jaws,

called **mandibles**, depend on the type of foods the beetle species eats. A wood-eating beetle needs stronger jaws than a beetle that drinks sap. Some beetles, like weevil species, have snouts similar to the noses found on echidnas or opossums. Rhino and stag beetles come equipped with horns,

Close up, this female tiger beetle looks like a monster from a horror movie.

abdomen   thorax   head

used for fighting, digging, and rooting out food. Beetle eyes are compound eyes with many **facets**, or lenses, called **ommatidia**. Beetle vision is limited, showing mostly size, shape, and motion. The antennae are sense organs, used in the same way the humans use their fingers.

The thorax is the power center of a beetle body. All six legs attach to the thorax, along with the two pairs of wings. Legs come in pairs—three pairs to each beetle, and each leg has five segments. Most beetles can tuck their legs under their bodies when they are under attack.

Beetles, such as this ceiba borer beetle, have three main body parts—head, thorax, and abdomen.

Beetle wings provide the beetle with flight and protection. The hard front pair of wings are called **elytra**. The elytra cover most of the beetle's body. They are made of chitin, a substance much like fingernails. Water beetles collect air under their elytra, while desert beetles collect dew, or the moisture that collects on surfaces overnight. In both cases, the beetles have used their elytra to help them adapt to a difficult environment.

The abdomen is where beetles have most of their major organs. Beetles digest food and get rid of waste through their abdomens. For beetles that spray acid at their enemies, such as bombardier beetles, the holding tank for the acid and the spraying organs reside in the abdomen. In addition, reproductive organs are found in the abdomen.

REPRODUCTION

Beetles, like bees and butterflies, undergo a complete **metamorphosis**. Most beetle species go through four stages in life: egg, larva, pupa, and adult. Females find the perfect spot for egg laying. This may be in soil, under decaying leaves, or in rotting wood. Sexton beetles use a dead animal's body for a nursery.

The number of eggs a female lays varies according to the species. Chafers will lay single eggs, while oil beetles deposit several thousand at a time. Beetle eggs are tiny, smooth, and soft.

A female stink beetle lays her eggs on a leaf.

When the eggs hatch, out comes beetle larvae, also called grubs. Larvae look like worms, wiggle like worms, and are generally about as appealing as worms. Larvae eat just about anything. Their main function is to eat, grow, molt—and repeat the process. The larvae usually have six simple eyes and well-developed mouthparts.

At the end of the larval stage, pupae receive a chemical signal from their bodies that say it is time to go through metamorphosis. Their bodies change from soft, sleek worms to fully developed adults during the pupa stage. Pupae cases or cells vary greatly, just as the beetles themselves do. Scarabs build pupae cells from soil, wood particles, and saliva. Diving beetles choose to dig into a river or lake bank. Wood boring beetle larvae drill tidy holes in soft or rotting wood as they feed. When it is time to enter the pupa stage, they just stop eating, and pupate in their personal feeding tunnels.

Emerging adults may look bland, but that appearance is temporary. As soon as their outer shells harden, their real colors appear: rich reds, vivid greens and blues, lush golds, brilliant oranges, and sleek, stunning blacks. Males and females may look identical, or they may have obviously different colorations.

Did You Know?
Beetle larvae eat a wide variety of foods: dead animals, dung, roots, leaf fibers, rotting fruits, and dead wood.

Adult beetles have one major goal in life: mating. They have a natural urge to reproduce, which is critical to keeping the

A stag beetle larva makes its home in a piece of wood.

species thriving. While some species of beetles survive a few short months, there are species that live up to 12 years.

PREDATORS

Hundreds of animal species—and a few select plants—feed on beetles. With so many beetle species, so many sizes, and so many habitats, nature needs to provide many and varied predators to control the beetle population. In deserts, lizards, snakes, rodents, and other insects munch on darkling beetles and other desert dwellers. Toads, frogs, fish, and waterfowl feast on beetles in fresh water ponds, lakes, and streams.

Birds and reptiles throughout the world are common beetle predators. Although beetles may come in super-sized models, like goliath beetles, they still have to deal with predators. A company of army ants will quickly dismember large beetles and haul the parts back to the colony for dinner.

Animals are not the only ones that feed on beetles. Carnivorous plants, like the sundew and the Venus flytrap, set their traps for beetles. They do not actually "eat" the beetles. They dissolve them and absorb their nutrients.

Chapter Three

Beetles, Beetles, and More Beetles

Beetles have existed for about 240 million years. They have outlasted fierce dinosaurs like *Tyrannosaurus rex* and powerful animals like saber-toothed tigers. With somewhere between 300,000 and 350,000 species, beetles make up 20 percent of all living organisms. In fact, these amazing creatures account for between one-fourth and one-third of all animals, and 40 percent of all insects.

Beetles succeed because they thrive in all sorts of places and eat all types of food. Other than the oceans and seas, all earth habitats have beetles. They live on land and in water, in the driest deserts and in the wettest rainforests. And, if the material is edible, there is a type of beetle that will eat it—fruit, vegetables, leaves, stems, roots, rotting wood, other insects, and rotting flesh. Beetles are plant eaters, meat eaters, and scavengers. Their ability to adapt allows them to survive in the harsh natural world.

All species of beetles have scientific names, such as *Poloposipus herculeanus* or *Nicrophorus americanus*. Many also have nicknames, common names by which their species are called: lightning bugs, weevils, June bugs, and ladybugs.

Some beetles are so beautifully and brightly colored that they are called living jewels. Others have what is called **cryptic** coloring. The coloring of these beetles blends in so well with their environment that they are hard to see. In both cases, coloring provides protection. Bright coloring usually warns of bad

A June bug's coloring allows it to "hide" on leaves.

Did You Know?
The heaviest beetle is the Goliath beetle, weighing up to 100 grams (3.5 ounces). The lightest beetle is the feather-winged beetle, which can weigh as little as 0.4 milligrams (0.006 grains).

taste or poison. Predators may eat one or two, but after a foul-tasting mouthful, they avoid catching similarly colored beetles. The cryptic coloring is camouflage. It makes finding a beetle difficult when in its natural environment.

Protective shells and the power of flight also protect beetles from becoming some other animal's dinner. The hard shell of beetles makes it difficult for many creatures to bite through their bodies. Tortoise beetles not only enjoy a hard shell, they also have an added defense. They can tuck their head and legs under their shells and hold fast to a leaf or branch. They ooze out a gluey substance that holds them securely to a surface. Ants, eager for a meal, try to push over the tortoise beetle with no success.

MAJOR BEETLE SUBORDERS

Scientists divide beetles into four major types, which are called suborders. Archostemata (AR-koh-steh-mah-tah) is an ancient group of beetles. These species date from 280 million years ago. Most of these species no longer exist. Records of these long-gone beetles appear in fossils, or the remains of these creatures preserved in rock.

Who Said That?
We went to all the places which a beetle
   might be near,
And we made the sort of noises which a
   beetle likes to hear,
And I saw a kind of something, and I gave
   a sort of shout:
"A beetle-house and Alexander Beetle
   coming out!"
—A. A. Milne, *The House at Pooh Corner*

The beetle suborder Myxophaga (MIX-oh-fa-guh) has only 22 species. These are tiny beetles found in tropical regions. Their larvae usually live in water, and they love hot, steamy weather.

The suborder Adephaga (AH-deh-fa-guh) consists of just over 30,000 species in 10 families. Most Adephaga beetles are meat eaters. They include tiger beetles, ground beetles, and beetles that thrive in the water (diving beetles, whirligig beetles, and screech beetles).

Whirligig beetles are one of the many beetle species in the Adephaga suborder.

Bombardier beetles, which belong to the Adephaga group, are chemical warriors. They spray predators with chemicals that burn skin and eyes. They carry their acid spray in their abdomens. When a predator nears, they point their bottoms at the enemy. A loud "pop" warns that the spray is on the way. Bombardier beetles chase away ants, toads, spiders, and birds with their painful spray.

A bombardier beetle isn't afraid to attack its enemies.

Three Cheers for Dung Beetles!

The average elephant produces 4 pounds (1.8 kilograms) of dung an hour—yes, pounds of dung! While most animals would walk carefully around elephant feces, dung beetles flock to the scene. Large dung beetles, such as Egypt's *Scarabaeus sacer,* roll dung into perfectly round balls in which they lay their eggs. Medium-sized dung beetles carry feces off in clumps. Tiny beetles may choose to remain in the dung pile, feeding on the nutrients in the feces. If nothing else, an elephant dung pile serves as a social club for dung beetles. One clump may feed or house up to 16,000 beetles from as many as 120 different species.

While many dung beetles pursue any type of feces, there are beetle species that specialize. For example, two uroxys beetles live in the fur of the three-toed sloth. Sloths live in South American rainforests, clinging to tree branches high in the canopy. Sloths eat, sleep, and live 30 meters (90 feet) or more above the forest floor. They go down to the forest floor to relieve themselves of waste—once every two or three weeks. Dung beetles clinging to sloth fur are on the spot when the sloth relieves itself. Other dung specialists include beetles that cling to kangaroos, howler monkeys, and wallabies, or beetles that dine only on dung from giraffes or wild pigs.

Among the water dwellers of the Adephaga group are predacious diving beetles. These beetles are strong swimmers, although they prefer shallow waters. Some predacious diving beetles are large enough to eat small fish. They may also dine on tadpoles, leeches, or snails. Their major protection is their flavor—they taste awful!

There is no insect suborder larger than the Polyphaga (PAH-lif-uh-guh) group with 248,000 species divided into 150 families. Add up all the species of butterflies, moths, ants, and bees, and they do not equal the number of Polyphaga beetles. These beetles can be found in every habitat, eating every type of food, and measuring every size from tiny to tremendous.

Some beetles in this group glow in the dark. Lightning bugs have what is called **bioluminescence**—they have chemicals in their systems that make them glow. Every species of lightning bug has its own flight pattern that it uses to attract a mate. Although most lightning bugs appear yellow, some glow green, blue, or orange.

Lightning bugs are predators, along with their relatives: hister beetles, ladybugs, and checkered beetles. Many of these species feed on tiny insects or rotting flesh.

Blister beetles are nature's hitchhikers. As young, they gather on the tip of a plant. A bee flies nearby, thinking that

A lightning bug—also called a firefly—uses its light to communicate.

the cluster of beetles is actually a blossom filled with nectar. The beetle young give off a scent to trick the bees into thinking they are flowers. The young blister beetles climb on the bee's back and hitch a ride to a new destination.

Many Polyphaga beetles feed on plant matter, and that includes leaves, stems, rotting wood, and fungus—a type of plant. The Colorado potato beetle has a serious reputation with potato farmers. These beetles can destroy an entire potato crop. Although potato plants are their favorite food, Colorado potato beetles are hardy species that thrive on many different plants.

Potato beetles can be found in many areas and live off a variety of crops.

Chapter Four

In Appreciation of Beetles

In ancient times, cave dwellers took lumps of coal and shaped them to look like beetles. They pierced the coal and hung the pendants from their necks. No one knows why, but since the days of early humans, beetles have fascinated humans.

The ancient Egyptians revered the beetle, using a dung beetle in its artwork. The insect is often shown clutching a golden disc between the claws. These beetles were known as scarabs and Egyptians painted images of them on pyramid walls and as decorations on ancient temples. Scarabs were even carved into the death mask of Tutankhamen, a famous ruler of Egypt.

Why were beetles so popular in ancient Egypt? The Egyptians connected the scarab beetle's life cycle to the life cycle of their main god, the sun god Ra. The beetles began their lives beneath the surface of the earth, just like the sun beneath the horizon. The beetle and the sun both rose from the earth. As the sun god Ra moved the sun across the sky, so did scarab beetles roll perfectly round dung balls across the ground.

The fascination Egyptians had for scarabs carried into their rites for the dead. Priests placed scarabs carved from soapstone, jade, or other kinds of stones on the chests of the dead. The scarabs represented the heart. They were thought to be the source of rebirth and immortality. Some scientists believe that mummies were wrapped to represent a beetle's metamorphosis, the change from one stage of life to the next stage.

The love of scarabs and beetles spread outward from Egypt. As the Persians, Greeks, and Romans overran Egypt, so did those cultures become interested in beetles. People began wearing gold or silver jewelry in the shape of beetles as good luck pieces.

In the Far East, the Japanese have long honored beetles in Horyuji Temple, in Nara, Japan. In the seventh century AD, a beetle shrine was built for Empress Suiko. Buddhist objects in the shrine feature more than 9,000 shining green beetle elytra.

Would You Believe?
Most natural history museums keep a collection of live dermestid (dur-MES-tid) beetles. These are flesh eaters used worldwide to clean animal skeletons. Take a skull, dump a pile of dermestid beetles on it, and a day or two later, the bones are spotless.

MYTHS AND LEGENDS

The Japanese also believe that golden beetles are a source of good luck. Place one on a wooden chest, and clothing would magically appear. In other cultures, legends claim that dor beetles placed on a money chest provided an endless source of money. For people in Bavaria, Germany, the head of a stag beetle on a chain represented good luck.

Scarab beetles can be found on many pieces of ancient Egyptian art and jewelry.

The French thought that stag beetles could carry burning embers from a fireplace. These innocent beetles were blamed for many house fires. No wonder French peasants killed stag beetles to ward off bad luck.

Unfortunately, early Christians also took a negative view of beetles. The Roman Catholic Church declared that beetles were foul and evil. People were told to keep away from beetles and never to think of them as symbols of good luck.

In France, some people believed that stag beetles brought bad luck.

BEETLES AROUND THE WORLD

Decorating with beetles seems a bit odd, but it is common among many native cultures. In the Amazon, glittering beetle wings decorate necklaces, earrings, and headdresses. In Mexico, large beetles create living jewels—literally. Colored glass and metal decorations are glued to the back of a live beetle, along with a chain. The beetle is held on clothing by the chain, but wanders around—a type of moving jewelry. The living jewel beetles recall an old Mayan legend. Once a prince was kept from his lover by her guards. The Moon Goddess turned him into a beetle, and he flew straight to his lover's side. The girl was impressed by his cleverness, and the two lived happily ever after. The living jewelry does not have quite as nice a life story. The beetles live for a few months in captivity, fed rotted wood, apples, and cereal by their owners.

Besides their decorative nature, humans have also used beetles as ingredients in medicines. In eighteenth-century Florence, ground weevil was a common cure for toothache. In nineteenth-century Europe, beetle grubs were believed to help nursing mothers produce milk. Dried, ground ladybugs were given to ease colic and the measles. Blister beetles provided relief from earaches and scorpion bites.

Modern medicine does not recommend dried, ground, powdered, or any other form of beetle as a cure for any disease. There is no proof that taking two beetles for any disease will do anything but provide a stomachache.

This ladybug is about to land on a plant.

Chapter Five

Man and Beetles

In 1830, a Mexican farmer discovered boll weevil larvae munching their way through his cotton crop. By 1892, boll weevils had reached the Rio Grande and crossed into Brownsville, Texas. From Arizona eastward, boll weevils invaded American cotton fields and laid waste to the most important crop in the South. Thousands of farmers lost everything—their crops, their farms, and all their money.

Although boll weevils may be well-known pesky beetles, they are not the only crop pests. Colorado potato beetles munch potato plants, while cigarette tobacco beetles chomp tobacco. Red-legged ham beetles prefer fatty foods—bacon, nuts, and cheese. The bamboo beetle is more of a general feeder. While it still chooses to make its way through bamboo furniture, it will also eat dried fruit, avocados, and cinnamon.

HUMANS USING BEETLES

Not all beetles are pests. Some can be downright helpful. Humans frequently

Did You Know?
The citizens of Enterprise, Alabama, lost a great deal when boll weevils destroyed cotton crops, but they learned a valuable lesson. They began to vary their farm crops, planting corn, potatoes, and peanuts. To honor the insect that inspired this change, the city erected a statue of a super-sized boll weevil.

make errors when it comes to nature, and beetles have been called on to fix up the messes. Whether planned or accidental, alien plant species have moved from continent

Boll weevils destroy cotton crops.

to continent. Those plants may have no natural element to balance their growth. Two such plant invaders are floating ferns and water hyacinths.

In 1972, some floating ferns arrived in Papua, New Guinea. Within eight years, mats of ferns clogged waterways, covered ponds, and damaged both fish and wildlife. The solution to floating ferns was a tiny weevil species. The adult weevils eat the actual ferns. The larvae devour large quantities of roots and stems.

Water hyacinths, like floating ferns, spread rapidly and block waterways. They reduce the fish population by blocking out sunlight and reducing the normal plant life common in a pond or river. Water hyacinths originated in Brazil but have spread to 53 countries. To get rid of the hyacinths using chemicals would be very expensive and would destroy many other plants and animals. Instead, the problem is being resolved by two other types of weevils.

Farmers also take advantage of hard-working beetles. Citrus beetles get rid of citrus scale, an insect species that attacks lemon, orange, grapefruit, and lime trees. Ladybugs help farmers get rid of aphids. Throughout the world, beetles are busily ridding us of insect pests, dung, and rotting animal carcasses.

The dung beetle is one of the many beetle species that helps the planet.

NATURE'S CYCLE OF LIVING THINGS

When a tree dies in the forest, it continues to provide life, food, and shelter. The tree falls to the forest floor and begins to rot. Dozens of beetle species lay their eggs within the rotting wood. As weeks pass, fungus and moss grow on the trunk, and more species feed on that growth. Borer beetle larvae munch tunnels into the decay and pupate within the wood. Small mammals, reptiles, and birds come to the log to feed on the insects living within the wood. Rain comes, decay increases, and the nutrients held in the tree seep into the ground. New plants grow, fed by the enriched soil. More beetle larvae feed on the young saplings. The cycle of life continues.

Beetles fulfill a critical role in nature. They are Mother Nature's recyclers, trash removers, and dung disposers. They feed on harmful insects, and yet can be harmful themselves. They are predators and prey, and far more plentiful than any other animal on Earth. Although humans are inclined to get rid of them, beetles work for us. Humans could not survive without them.

Glossary

abdomen (AB-doh-mehn) the elongated portion of the body of an arthropod, located behind the thorax

antennae (an-TEN-nee) thin, sensory organs found on the heads of many insects

bioluminescence (bye-oh-loo-mih-NESS-sense) the generation of light by a living organism, such as a lightning bug

cryptic (KRIP-tik) body markings and colors that camouflage an animal

elytra (EL-ih-truh) protective wings of a beetle; the singular is *elytron* (eh-LIH-trahn)

facets (FAA-setz) the separate lenses that make up an insect's eye

feces (FEE-sees) solid waste of an animal

larva (LAHR-vuh) wormlike life stage of insects that develop into the pupa stage; the plural is *larvae* (LAHR-vee)

mandibles (MAN-dih-bulz) the jaw parts of an insect's mouth

metamorphosis (meht-uh-MOR-foh-sis) a complete change in body form as an animal changes into an adult

ommatidia (ahm-uh-TIH-dee-uh) the visual facets, or lenses, of an insect eye

pupa (PYOO-puh) the insect stage during which an immature larva develops into an adult; the plural is *pupae* (PYOO-pee)

thorax (THOR-aks) the middle division of an insect, crustacean, or spider

For More Information

Watch It

Beetles & Spiders, DVD. (Los Angeles: Delta Entertainment, 2001.)

Creatures of the Namib Desert, VHS. (Washington, D.C.: National Geographic, 1998.)

GeoKids: Chomping on Bugs, Swimming Sea Slugs, and Stuff that Makes Animals Special, VHS. (Washington, D.C.: National Geographic, 1994.)

Read It

Claybourne, Anna. *Beetles and Other Bugs*. Mankato, Minn.: Stargazer Books, 2004.

Miller, Sara Swan. *Beetles: The Most Common Insects*. Danbury, Conn.: Franklin Watts, 2000.

Pascoe, Elaine. *Nature Close-Up: Beetles*. Farmington Hills, Mich: Blackbirch Press, 2001.

Penny, Malcolm. *Beetles*. Chicago: Raintree, 2003.

Twist, Clint. *Dung Beetles*. Milwaukee, Wisc.: Gareth Stevens, 2005.

Look It Up

Visit our Web site for lots of links about beetles:
http://www.childsworld.com/links

Note to Parents, Teachers, and Librarians: We routinely verify our Web links to make sure they are safe, active sites—so encourage your readers to check them out!

The Animal Kingdom
Where Do Beetles Fit In?

Kingdom: Animal

Phylum: Arthropoda

Class: Insecta

Order: Coleoptera

Genus and Species: 300,000 to 350,000 species

Index

About the Author

Sophie Lockwood is a former teacher and a longtime writer. She writes textbooks, newspaper articles, and magazine articles. Sophie enjoys writing about animals and their habits. The most interesting part of her research, Sophie says, is learning how scientists apply their knowledge to save endangered species. She lives with her husband in the foothills of the Blue Ridge Mountains.